BORN STILL BUT NOT SILENT

Born Still but Not Silent

A collection of poems

by

CYNTHIA A. DITARANTO

Adelaide Books
New York / Lisbon
2020

To Sonya

and her world of stillness, for it is in this world of stillness where my answers were found.

and

to all the empty cradles…………..

and

the rest of my family

BORN STILL BUT NOT SILENT
A collection of poems
By Cynthia A. DiTaranto

Copyright © by Cynthia A. DiTaranto
Cover design © 2020 Adelaide Books

Published by Adelaide Books, New York / Lisbon
adelaidebooks.org

Editor-in-Chief
Stevan V. Nikolic

All rights reserved. No part of this book may be reproduced in any manner whatsoever without written permission from the author except in the case of brief quotations embodied in critical articles and reviews.

For any information, please address Adelaide Books
at info@adelaidebooks.org
or write to:
Adelaide Books
244 Fifth Ave. Suite D27
New York, NY, 10001

ISBN: 978-1-953510-24-2

Printed in the United States of America

Illustrations:
Cover: photo of an acrylic painting by author *4*
Sonya's gravesite: photo taken by author *38*
Photo of an angel drawing by Adam DiTaranto *42*
Photo of an angel statue in a bleeding heart patch taken by author *52*
Photo of a Victorian Mourning Pin taken by author *59*

"Sadness is but a wall between two gardens."
Khalil Gibran

Contents

Introduction **13**

Who Am I? **17**

State of Nothingness **18**

Expectations **19**

The Room **20**

State of Unhappiness **21**

She is Still **22**

The Day **25**

The Experience **25**

No Way **26**

Vanished Hope **26**

Again and Again **26**

Dark Spring **27**

Unexpected *27*

Boil, Boil…….. *28*

Why Me? *29*

Envy *29*

Return to Stardust *30*

Time In-between *31*

Pain of Loss *32*

Void *33*

Who Died? *34*

Still Birth *36*

Still Born *36*

Eyes *37*

What is Her Name? *37*

Where is She? *37*

Found *39*

Rendering *40*

Guardian *41*

Overheard *41*

The Messenger *42*

Lullaby *43*

Fire Red *44*

Is it Contagious? *45*

Faultless *46*

Scattering *47*

Birthdays *48*

I Stand Exposed *49*

Danger in the Air *51*

The Bleeding Heart *53*

Handless Maiden *54*

Labyrinth *55*

From the Center *57*

Far but Near *57*

Ask Her Name *58*

Keepsake *59*

Finding Serenity *60*

Evolution *61*

Grace *62*

Knowing *62*

Transforming **63**

From Another Time **64**

Even Now **65**

No Answers **66**

Today **67**

She's Mine to Know **68**

Love Letter **69**

She Lives **70**

Who Would She Be? **71**

Becoming **72**

I Am **73**

Completeness **74**

Conclusion **75**

Acknowledgements **77**

About the Author **79**

Introduction

My journey is a woman's journey. I once mistakenly told a friend that I belonged to a unique group of women that have a special knowledge. My path to this "knowing" led me to give birth to a stillborn daughter. This was my path but not the only path. The wisdom of this "knowing—a journey into stillness" awaits all who seek it. It is not a place to be feared, for here, like a phoenix rising a true rebirth can begin.

How did I come to the realization that this wisdom is not reserved for an exclusive group? Once I started to evolve as a person, I reached a point where my world expanded so greatly that I delighted in having reached the apex. I was most assuredly mistaken. My work had just begun. As soon as I became ecstatic with successfully reaching a higher state of understanding, my ego swelled filling up an empty vat. The vat started to leak. My arrogance was struck down as quickly as it surfaced. I found myself on a plateau on which to rest while I became accustomed to the new territory. Then, I ventured to evolve further. Every time I basked in the aura of my new awareness, the vat began to leak and I plateaued. The process repeated itself over and over plunging me deeper and deeper into my subconscious and, at the same time, expanding my awareness out into the universe.

I quieted my mind and listened. Here, I discovered my inherent nature: the place where life begins and ends/the place where life ends and begins; the connection to the female innate province; the place of the eternal cycle. Some women are born with this knowledge. Some find it early in life. Some resist its presence. Some are fearful of it. Some struggle to its awareness. Some discover only part of it. There is no right or wrong. There is only the personal journey.

Women do not sit around and discuss this subject. They share this profound understanding through unspoken communication. In a fleeting moment, it can be seen deep in a woman's eyes or in her body language: the nod of her head, the way she extends her hand, in her tears, in her smile, the tone of her voice, in the manner in which she listens. The place of knowing—the place of stillness—is not stagnant.

I was born knowing. I quickly lost it. I spent the rest of my life trying to find it. As with most things, I found it in quite unusual places. Like Alice in her adventures in wonderland, I fell into my own rabbit hole. Like the Red Queen, I had to run as fast as I could to keep up. Then, I stopped running. I stood still and fell into silence. I found comfort there. I became wiser there. I grew and expanded. I became part of what is larger than all of us and connected to that which we are all connected to. My perspectives changed; my being shifted. I was ready to begin to understand the eternal life cycle: life to death—vibrancy to stillness; death to life—stillness to vibrancy.

I returned from the quiet. I wanted to share and connect with others: to validate, to comfort, to reach out, and to hold hands with those who will or have taken the journey into stillness. I invite you to step through the doorway with me as I continue to experience the impact of giving birth to a daughter

BORN STILL BUT NOT SILENT

born still so many years ago. The year was 1976. I was not given the opportunity to bond with my deceased infant. She was whisked away and hushed voices made her final arrangements. Her fetal death certificate bears no first name.

Who Am I?

A woodsman came.
He took an ax and split me in two.
Me before.
Me after.

State of Nothingness

Emptiness

No sense of smell

The taste of unsalted food

A bell without a gong

Being lost in space

The universe's biggest black hole

Emptiness

Expectations

Surprise, surprise!
It was to be for mother and babe to be.
Raining gifts wrapped with care,
Piled high around the wishing well:
Play pen, swing and high chair bring oohs and aahs,
Everything required--a complete layette.

The awaited time is oh so near.
Everyone waits with joy and cheer,
For no one foretells what sadness will befall
When nine months end and the child is born dead.
Only offers of sympathy and condolences will do.

The Room

Lemon chiffon nursery, rich coffee brown décor,
Hand painted mural adorning one wall.

Refurbished crib from long ago.
Cross stitch quilts made with love.

Drawers filled with cute outfits but oh so small,
Little stuffed toys so cuddly and soft.

Musical mobile waiting to be wound
But for a long time, never makes a sound.

For no infant comes to inhabit this space.
It lies empty and falls out of grace.

Sitting quiet, falling from view,
Waiting patiently for someone new.

State of Unhappiness

Sadness

The scent of perfume years past its expiration date

The taste of chili without spices

A chorus of croaking bull frogs

Falling into a deep, dark crevice

A lone stranded survivor of a ship wreck

Sadness

She is Still

Influential as it
May be
The full moon glows bright
For all to see.

Although found by some
Skeptically,
No more than a myth
Without authenticity.

The lunar effects
Remain unchanged,
Exerting her force,
The earth enthroned.

Pressure begins,
The rise and fall.
Contractions follow
Very rhythmical.

Anticipation of the womb
Yielding its hold
On a new life
So we are told.

Something is not right
Something is wrong.

BORN STILL BUT NOT SILENT

There is no cry
No baby's song.

The sound of silence
Fills the air.
The pain is oh
So much to bear!

My precious child
No matter what I will
Does not move
For she is still.

I fall away
Behind a veil.
Time has stopped,
Can't they tell?

I am transformed
Forever more
By the child I
Cry out for.

My child, my life will
Remain with me
Throughout
All eternity.

We journey together,
Our paths not clear,

Cynthia A. DiTaranto

Gifts uncovered,
Letting go of the fear.

I look out at the pale
Moonlight.
Her phases changing
Each and every night.

The full moon waning
Hiding its light,
Becoming new, waxing again
Full and bright.

The numinous wonder and I
Do share,
Life's secrets of which
We are the heir.

The Day

June third, the day my life changed.
Ushered into a twilight zone,
Shriveled into a cocoon,
Fighting off dread and doom,
Time came to a halt.
This can't be real.
Shock took hold.
I'm scared.
Help

The Experience

No heartbeat
Fear
Panic
Uncontrollable trembling

Continue labor
Drugs
Haze
Forceps pulling

Slip behind time
Shock
Detach
Dissociative amnesia

Fall asleep
Dreams
Frightened
Reality check

No place to turn
Grief
Plead
Find answers

No Way

In a daze
I see her outline.
She coaxes me
to push.
I want to but don't succeed.
Forceps.

> Vanished Hope
>
> I am in labor.
> I wonder what is happening.
> I hear dread in their voices.
> I smell fear oozing from their bodies.
> I see nothing but a blur around me.
> I feel panic rising like suffocating smoke.
> I taste a metallic taste of doom.
> I try to control my quivering to no avail.
> I believe my world has forever changed.
> I understand I hold death within me.
> I am in labor.

Again and Again

In and out they rush.
Monitor—try; then, once more.
No heartbeat is found.

Dark Spring

Spring brings renewal.
    I anticipate her birth.
        No heartbeat or breath.

        Unexpected

        Birth I expected.
           Birth I gave.
              Life I expected.
                  Death came.

Boil, Boil……..

The cauldron brews life
And death from which all
That is born returns.

Memories ferment
Within my world—too
Long they remain.

Agitate—provoke—exasperate.
Bubble and boil, spill over,
No longer contained.

The abscess has broken,
The pustule bursts,
The infection is released.

Why Me?

The special are chosen.
Isn't that so?
Not always it seems.
On what criteria did you judge
To choose a woman
To birth death?
Bringing forth life is joyous.
Death is full of sorrow.
No one deserves such pain.
Yet the Great Mother knows all.

Envy

I watch
moms with their babes
walking in the park
while I sit on a bench
alone.

Return to Stardust

The stars shinning
    so bright
In the dim
    moonlight.

Gazing into the
    vastness,
Hearing the
    stillness.

Contemplating the
    thought,
The answers
    I sought.

If to dust
    we return,
Is the theory
    so firm,

As not
    to suggest
That our
    eternal quest,

Connects
    to entrust,
Our return
    to stardust.

Time In-between

Time in-between holds mysteries untold.
The secret space where no one can go
As long as death is not our foe.
Will the loss of breath be so bold
To expose what's contained within this fold?
Only the whispering wind does know.
Time in-between

And what of the one born still and cold,
Has she slipped into the crevice formed long ago
Along with my grief and sorrow?
The answers are held in this strong hold.
Time in-between

Pain of Loss

Grief

Gaging on the stench of an unclean latrine

Tasting your own vomit

Sounding the death knell

Being lost in the wilderness

Gazing at a garden of dead flowers

Grief

Void

I fell off a cliff; do not tell me it's okay. I'm already falling.

I've fallen behind a veil. I am no longer part of your world.

If you send bouquets, stick an artificial
flower in them to represent me.

I bleed where no one can see, beneath my
skin. An arrow has pierced my heart.

Time has stopped. Didn't you get the memo?

I fell down Alice's rabbit hole. Nothing makes sense.

Exposed, standing naked on the freeway. I don't care.

Who Died?

I feel like I have died—part of me did.
My loss is so enormous,
I don't know who I am anymore.
My arms hang limp—no cradle to form.
I am miserable and there's no place to hide.
How can my heart be breaking so?

The nursery remains just so.
A constant reminder of what I did,
Gave birth to a dead child, a fact I cannot hide.
What do I do with this burden so enormous?
Time has frozen; my life has no form.
Is there any reason to care anymore?

I don't know how to cope anymore.
I have no reason to get through a day, so
I do nothing for life has no shape or form.
But wait! A headstone we created—we most certainly did,
Granting serenity so enormous,
It lifts me from where I hide.

There must be something to grab onto whatever the form,
A warm breeze finds me for I no longer hide.
Someone tells me to take it slow and I did.
I'm done with tears. There aren't anymore.
"Light a candle—the darkness will melt," my friend says so.
A breakthrough would be enormous.

BORN STILL BUT NOT SILENT

Your connection is eternal and your love enormous.
There are others who understand and stand true to form.
What we choose to focus on is the catalyst for how long we
Despair; it is so.
Don't need to struggle alone anymore.
Joined a support group is what I did.

The gift I received was enormous; no use of any dark well
In which to hide.
I picture my daughter in angelic form
as my teacher, my guide,
And I'm not afraid anymore.
I've reached out to others who have suffered so; their journey
May begin like mine did.

Still Birth

Slumber, my darling, in everlasting sleep.
Today, I begin to mourn.
Immersed in unspeakable grief,
Life existing inside my womb?
Labor begins in the wee hours of the night.

Born Breathless, you will be.
Impaled is my heart for my baby that lays still.
Repeat what you said. How can there be no heart beat?
Tossed into a tailspin, losing all control.
Hush now, I'm told; all traces of evidence
       concealed out of sight.

Still Born

Sleeping is fitful from which I awake.
Time has no meaning locked in a world of my own.
It wasn't a dream, so where did she go?
Longing for answers, I'm told where to head.
Locked on a mission, we find where she rests.

Building our own monument to honor her soul,
Our daughter is real in spite of being born still.
Relief in being able to say goodbye,
No one can tell me her existence was not tangible.

Eyes

Blue, green, brown or black,
    That knowledge is something I lack.

        What is Her Name?

      No name will not do.
          Identity makes her real.
         I call her Sonya.

Where is She?

Whispers in the night
    become shouts.
        I wake and must know.

Found

A sacred haunt for tiny graves,
So many! I did not know the peace between the rows.
Pennies scattered for their delight,
Kneel down to honor their little souls.
It's here the quiet sings to me
Like a magical symphony.
Without words we converse,
Otherworlds transversed.

Rendering

Angel
Ephemeral   Guardian
Watching   Comforting   Listening
A daughter, a sister, an infant born still.
A child's ability to bridge the boundaries of two worlds.
Expressing   Personifying   Symbolizing
Childlike   Sincere
Drawing

Guardian

Never far; she's always near.
From worlds beyond protection comes
As she guards us from her celestial sphere
Granting a sense of freedom.

Whenever trouble looms for someone dear,
I beseech her help with my problems.
She never fails to engineer
A plan to transform woes into blossoms.

Overheard

Babes converse.
Inquiry formed.
Without hesitation,
Response spoken out loud.
I have a sister
said casually but proud.
She is an angel.

The Messenger

Angel
She is.
The answer to: why?
Connect the dots……
Direct line to the divine.

Lullaby

When the beginning and end get mixed up,
And death slips in to steal you away,
Nothing else matters or can compare
To the precious life I lost that day.

I'm told you were fair with peach fuzz for hair.
At first, I was lost 'til you sent me strength.
You are not here; yet you are.
We are forever joined—on the same wavelength.

Now you are carried in my heart,
Safe from anything that can harm.
My first born child cherished still,
Protecting from above, my tiny good luck charm.

I'm told you were fair with peach fuzz for hair.
At first, I was lost 'til you sent me strength.
You are not here; yet you are.
We are forever joined—on the same wavelength.

Fire Red

Anger

The charred smell of burning flesh

Chocking on a serving of spoiled fish

The rumbling of a stamping herd of buffalo

A brain aneurism

Watching a town crumple under a bomb attack

Anger

Is it Contagious?

Disease
Infectious   transmittable
Disseminate   Protect   Isolate
Harmful influence, I can't stay near
Snub her presence and move away
Detest   Repulse   Disgust
Unsympathetic   Antipathetic
Aversion

Faultless

I failed as woman to usher forth a life.
What culprit stole my genders rightful glory?
For what have I done causing hopes to take flight?
I'm hard on myself; others aren't accusatory.
When stillbirth knocks, no fault can find a target.
For sure, it was not part of any bargain.
Anomalies appear mysteriously,
Their purpose hidden most nefariously.

Scattering

Women congregate.
Storytelling can't wait.
My turn to share; I hesitate.

Heads turn,
Mine burns,
Looks of concern.

First birth I fear,
Not one to cheer,
Stillborn my dears.

Silence prevails,
No request for details,
Women retreat like snails.

Birthdays

It took a so long to celebrate,
Her death was mine and mine was hers,
The date of birth and death the same,
Was no way to rejoice in giving birth.

Hers/mine what difference does it make?
I am empty, my life force drained.
My earthly arrival, how insignificant,
When baby's born without a breath.

Neither candles for me nor any for her,
For my wish, if I could blow upon the candle's glow
Will never have a chance of coming true—
The gift of life snuffed out too.

For many years I have no desire
To hear the song sung in birth's honor.
On that day sadness looms,
My being entwined with yours.

I Stand Exposed

The world takes on
An eerie glow,
As the veil of moonlight
Casts its spell below.

I'm not safe
As I stand exposed.
The shadows lurk
As my mind's functions are slowed.

Who am I now?
What will I become?
I hope for the best.
I'm put to the test.

I shift and change.
Is this to be my plight?
I dwindle away
Into the stillness of night.

I am fraught
With despair.
No way to mend,
No way to repair.

I seek out others
With whom to connect,

Cynthia A. DiTaranto

For here, I find those
That will accept.

Clothed by these wings
Of support,
I find untouched resources of strength
To which I resort.

I must cross the bridge
Both forward and back,
Until I find peace
So that I won't seep through the cracks.

Danger in the Air

Fear

The taste of blood

The wail of prey dying

The feel of adrenaline rushing through veins

The sight of a rabbit just before it's caught in an eagle's talons

Fear

The Bleeding Heart

The bleeding heart
Sheds a tear
For sadness felt
Both far and near.

Gather round the
Garden gate.
Linger, rest but
Most of all communicate.

Share your troubles,
Fears and grief.
Together we will find
Relief.

Handless Maiden

My psyche wounded; inward I retreat,
Pulling the covers secure, my grief crawls in beside me.
Somewhere deep the pain expands like
hot air inflating a balloon.
Experience petrifies; unrelenting, life journeys on.
For years, the cauldron burns and boils,
Visions float, rising.....rising—oh, please stop.

Legs tremble—can others hear?
Hands pressed upon them to no avail.
I taste the fear; I feel the fear; I am the fear.
Tampered brakes—losing control,
Holding breath—too late,
My face reveals my tremendous anxiety.

No amount of riot gear contains the overflow,
Handless Maiden—your myth slays open buried wounds.
Last sense of aliveness comes to roost.
Your silver hands useless to save your babe,
Yet, still you thrust handless limbs into the stream
And so reclaim what you thought you'd lost.

Your tale awakes my sleeping fears.
I broke down like a tired old truck,
Born anew with what they called a breakthrough.
Sacred surroundings—St. Marguerite's,
I thrust down my heavy bag of burdens.
With release comes peace.

Labyrinth

Women flank me in protective folds.
"You need to walk the labyrinth,
Over there, you must go alone,
Bring the soul into focus."

You need to walk the labyrinth,
A journey through the maze,
Bring the soul into focus,
Up from the depths, subconscious rises.

A journey through the maze—
Blocked path; try another.
Up from the depths, subconscious rises,
Into my internal depths, I silently fall.

Blocked path; try another,
Stray branch—bend and remove.
Into my internal depths, I silently fall,
Round and round circles shrink.

Stray branch—bend and remove,
Pause and listen to silence that I hear.
Round and round circles shrink,
The center calls and beckons me in.

Pause and listen to silence that I hear.
What voice speaks to me?

Cynthia A. DiTaranto

The center calls and beckons me in.
"Look up," requests the never world.

What voices speak to me?
From deep within; from places unseen,
"Look up," request the never world.
There is what I came to see.

From deep within; from places unseen,
I feel her presence; she is there with me.
There is what I came to see,
A large oak tree—in my sight.

A swing sways ever gracefully.
"Over there, you must go alone."
Until my child comes to me,
Women flank me in protective folds.

From the Center

No fallen leaves rustle;
Empty swing sways on bare branch.
Her spirit appears.

        Far but Near

        I hear her tender distant voice.
        I smell the fresh scent of washed linen.
        I see deep into her soul.
        I feel her presence around me.
        I taste her sweetness.

Ask Her Name

Do not remain afraid to share my pain,
But please refrain from speaking coarse clichés.
Just hold my hand to break the strain,
Support me 'til despair and sorrow pass.

How great if someone thinks to ask her name!
Our daughter grants the titles Mom and Dad,
Yes, parents for sure, I will exclaim—
A fact to speak out loud, of which I'm glad.

Her life remains for keeps entwined with mine
Despite how many years have passed on by.
A trigger wakens wounds, no doubt a sign,
Again I suffer from my pain and loss.

They ask how many children have you?
One birth was still but living children two.

Keepsake

Mourning Pin
Victorian   Photo
Sharing   Borrowing   Healing
A gift to borrow pretending it's my own.
Soon another child grows. Will the sun shine or weeds grow?
Knowing   Interceding   Nurturing
Compassionate   St. Elizabeth Ann Seton
Prayer Card

Finding Serenity

Peacefulness

The scent of Earth after a gentle rain

Lingering tastes of fabulous flavors

Debussy played on a harp

Experiencing a sacred space

Gazing up into a clear blue, cloudless sky

Peacefulness

Evolution

Under the light
    of the new moon,
Begin anew.
        It is time to bloom.

Full moon looming
    as big as can be,
Retreat! For it's time
        To be quiet, you see.

One night radiating bright
    under the moon glow,
Playing hide and seek
        with clouds both high and low.

Changing as it
    travels.
Accepting what it
    reveals.

For as all journey's
    paths proceed,
Evolution is the call
        we must heed.

Grace

Granting me strength to hold to my convictions
Refusing to be denied my right to motherhood
Accepting Sonya's death with dignity
Confronting myself to find the answers
Expanding my vision to see beyond my limited borders

Knowing

Knowledge—the path to stillness where rebirth begins
Nature—the place where life begins and ends;
    where life ends and begins
Open heart; hear the silence
Women gather together; closing ranks; protecting
Inner peace—home of innate power—the
    solitude and stillness of femininity
Nurturing ourselves and others with understanding of eternity
Gratitude—born still but not silent

Transforming

My daughter gave birth to me.
Arriving like a painting of a pear,
Silence pierced the air,
And at some point, I vicariously died.

But though the fog descended on the horizon,
In time, it cleared and I arose
Transformed forever. I continued underground.
Like a sleeping volcano, I bide time.

My psyche never quite satisfied.
Her energy reabsorbed remains like a time release capsule.
Each hit propelling forward,
To understand the meaning of life's cycle.

Left in the wake of her stillness,
I have grown.

From Another Time

Other women have shared my fate—
A child's birth and death in unison.
Frozen, I stare in disbelief—
I share in their grief.
After all these years….
What I see brings back the tears.

Searching ghosts of buried ancestors,
Coaxing out those left behind,
And there it is that I find,
Once, twice—so many times.
We never met; yet we have,
Suffering present or past—time has no frame.

I feel alone; yet I am not.
Unspoken words cannot erase,
The secret spot inside my soul,
Left empty—deprived of a part of you, a part of me.
Questions—Chasing answers,
I take a look back.

Comfort, odd as it may seem,
Found in such honorable company.
I find myself starring at your names,
Feeling a special affinity.
For all mothers who have known such grief,
Close ranks sharing in one community.

Even Now

Again and again, I read a book,
Shock value added with the same hook.
So many chapters all to fill their pocketbooks.

Women bear a child born still
With more words the page to fill,
No depth to the pain, they lift the quill.

How many readers have been there?
The written words reviving emotions bare.
Recent or past, we've no time to prepare.

Do not shy away from delving deep.
Write our story even if we weep.
Give homage to those born asleep.

No Answers

I searched everywhere:
    behind a door,
        under a rock,
            amongst the clouds.

I asked everyone:
    the doctors,
        friends and family,
            keepers of the faith.

I explored my territory high and low.
I rummaged through my beliefs.
I scrutinized my behaviors,
Like a child's insistent questioning.

I asked why? Why? Why"
But like my daughter……
Their lips remained still.

Today

As years pass by,
And I'm no longer spry,
I have no need to quantify
The existence of my little Gemini.
She comes with such purity,
Before long we'll meet in Shanghai.
Time has served to clarify.
I no longer ask why.

She's Mine to Know

No one else will ever know
Who the child is I grew in my womb.

I felt your heart beat rhythmically
And your tiny feet kick insistently.

I fed you through the food I ate,
We shared what was on my dinner plate.

Nine months we lived as one
Sharing everything bar none.

I never got to see your face,
But I know you no matter the place.

We'll always share a special bond,
Here on Earth and beyond.

I know you hear my every word.
My conversations do not go unheard.

You will forever be
A special child that came to me.

Love Letter

Forever, I will hold you in my heart

Full of love for one my arms cried out for.

'Til time can no longer keep us apart,

Forever, I will hold you in my heart.

How I longed for you from the start,

In a blink, I will know you once more.

Forever, I will hold you in my heart

Full of love for one my arms cried out for.

She Lives

She's far; yet near.
She's silent; yet loquacious.
She's still; yet busy.
She's mute; yet enlightening.
She's expressionless; yet articulate.
She's dead; yet alive.

Who Would She Be?

A conjured image
    has its limits.
An imagined deportment
    allows for a wide assortment.
A contrived list of milestones
    whirl through like a cyclone.

Becoming

On your next birthday,
Forty three is what you'd be.
For all those years that have passed away,
I pretend that I can foresee.

A kind hearted, soft soul,
Or a warrior filled with fire.
Over these I had no control
As to what you would aspire.

Fair complexion I was told—
Peach fuzz in place of hair.
No matter what, you would be bold,
For you are one that is so rare.

An act of nature or did you choose
Not to stay upon this plane?
Whatever reason, I can't refuse,
To know you did not die in vain.

A girl of courage and without fear,
Like a wise old sage,
To teach a lesson, I had to submit.
Time is short; decide what you hold dear.

If you had stayed,
A free spirit I see,
Not accepting any blockade,
In order to find the master key.

I Am

Has my chance passed me by?
Oh motherhood! A sacrament of love, none other so great.
Without a babe to hold, is it a title I surrender
Like a prisoner relinquishing breathing fresh air?
No. Two babes I have born. All three forever bound.
I am their Mother.
I am proud.

Completeness

Under the light of the Blue Moon

The wise woman gazes into the depths of
the water that spreads out before her.

In the silence of the night her soul is reflected back.

She now has the knowledge from the
words that could not be spoken.

Her womanhood epitomizes the delicate balance:

The miracle of birth; the tragedy of death without separation.

Others fear the possibility; they turn away.

They mustn't see their moonlit shadow.

The wise woman reaches upward to embrace the moon.

She cannot turn aside.

She was chosen!

Forever after, she bears the knowledge
of the light and the dark.

A moonbeam enshrines her radiance.

She is complete.

Conclusion

The experience of a stillbirth delivery, provided me with an understanding of the words that do not need to be spoken—a grasping of the exchange of energies between life and death—a knowing. Once I acknowledged this gift, I embarked on a journey that culminated in an all-encompassing understanding of eternity as myself being part of it in the present moment. The knowing led me to a place of forgiveness and compassion which I used to heal myself and to out to others. My road was not straight. It curved, and forked and had many bumps and ruts that I fell into. But I journeyed on.

Ironically, I ended up with what I was running from—stillness. The road led me inward to the place of my innate power—the solitude and stillness of my inner femininity. I took the risk and I found that my child who was born still had most certainly had not been born in silence.

Acknowledgements

My family for filling my life with joy.

To all those who have offered their condolences and comfort.

To the Adelaide book team for their expertise in designing a book I am proud of.

To my editor, Stevan B. Nikolic who saw poetic beauty shining through tragedy.

Thank you.

About the Author

Cynthia A. DiTaranto holds a Bachelor of Arts degree in sociology from Upsala College in East Orange, New Jersey where she graduated magna cum laude and a Master of Arts in Teaching that she received from Fairleigh Dickerson University in Teaneck, New Jersey. Her eclectic work related experience in N.J. includes: working as a licensed real estate agent; teaching history at Sparta High School; being a former part owner of Flanders Valley Farms, a catering facility and Little Sleepy Hollow Farm where she breed and sold champion Nigerian dwarf goats; serving as one of the managing members of Roxbury Enterprises, L.L.C. She is a certified hypno-counselor, a certified master neuro linguistic practitioner and trainer and a Reiki master. In addition, she is a member of the International Medical and Dental Hypnotherapy Association and a member of the American Goat Society. As a volunteer, she served as a brownie leader and as a participant of the Roxbury Historical Advisory Committee in Roxbury Township, New Jersey. Her time as a volunteer at Morris County's shelter for battered women and her committed time as a Reiki practitioner at the Carol G. Simon Cancer Center at Morristown Memorial Hospital in Morristown, New Jersey were invaluable experiences. Retired and residing in New Jersey with her husband, her creative side has been given its freedom. Reading, writing and painting fills her artistic space. Cynthia is the author of two self-published, color illustrated children's books: *Top Of The Heap* and *Kristmas Karol, The Nigerian Dwarf Goat*. She has written for various goat journals such as *Dwarf Digest* where her breeder profile entitled, *Written In The Stars* appeared and her article, *Experiences In Life Taught By A Pygmy*, was printed in United Caprine News. Her memoir piece, *Bloom*, has been published in *Narrative Northeast Literary and Art Review* and her fiction short story, *The Violinist*, appeared in a *Goldfinch Literary Journal*, a literary journal of Women Who Write, Inc. *Down in the Dirt* (an anthology) published another one of her fiction short stories, *Escape,* and *Joy,* an interpretative piece appears in *With Painted Words* (literary magazine). In *Synesthesia Literary Journal* the reader will find her poem, *The Synesthete*. She is a member of the Art Association of Roxbury; The Write Stuff, a writing workshop in Chester, New Jersey. Her women's fiction novel, *Flying High*, will soon be published by Dreaming Big.

 Giving birth to a stillborn daughter was a life changing event that has become part of who she is. Her struggle with grief was silent until it refused to remain so. As she evolved, she learned that the life experiences she breathed in could be exhaled through her writing and painting. *Born Still but Not Silent* is her first collection of poetry that tells her stillbirth story. It has waited in the shadows before it pushed its way to the surface. With a life of its own, *Born Still but Not Silent* decided on the right format and time to be published. The language of poetry reached into the soul of what she wanted to convey: an understanding of the eternal life cycle—life to death-vibrancy to stillness; death to life-stillness to vibrancy.

www.ingramcontent.com/pod-product-compliance
Lightning Source LLC
Chambersburg PA
CBHW020232090426
42735CB00010B/1658